# A.M.P.

## Amplify your Growth and Re-Energize your Business

Valter Klug

**Preface**....................................................................................................10

**Introduction:**
**The Great Growth Stall**.............................................................12

    Assessment: Exposing the blind spots that are holding you back...............................................................................................13

    Success Story: The Sleeping Giant........................................ 14

**Chapter 1:**
**Assessment**
**- Exposing Your Blind Spots**.................................................... 15

    Where Growth Goes to Die........................................................16

    Case Study: The Missed Opportunity....................................17

    The A.M.P. Audit. .........................................................................17

    Getting into Action..................................................................... 17

    Exercise: The 5 Whys.................................................................19

    Get Ready to Get Uncomfortable.......................................... 19

**Chapter 2:**
**Mindset**
**– Breaking Free from "How We've Always Done It"**.............. 20

    The Innovation Killers.............................................................. 21

    Case Study: Hispanic Food Company.................................. 22

    Cultivating a Growth Mindset................................................ 22

    Exercise: The Innovation Blindspot Audit............................23

    The Power of Disruption...........................................................23

    Adapting to the New Normal: Business Strategies Post-COVID-19..............................................................................23

        Key Lesson #1: Agility is the New Superpower...................24

    Key Lesson #2: Digital Isn't Optional, It's the Foundation.... 24

    Key Lesson #3: The Human Connection Matters More Than Ever...............25

    Resilience = Reinvention...............25

    Health & Safety: The Trust Factor...............26

    The World is Open for Business (Again) – Are You Ready?...............26

## Chapter 3:
## Market Analysis
## - Seeing the Unseen...............27

    Where Growth Opportunities Hide...............28

    Case Study: Juice Brand...............29

    Data-Driven Discovery...............29

    Exercise: Crafting Your U.S. Customer Persona...............30

    Beyond the Obvious...............30

## Chapter 4:
## Positioning
## - Finding Your Untapped Advantage...............31

    The Problem with Blending In...............32

    The Power of Differentiation...............32

    Case Study: Refreshment Beverage...............33

    Rediscover Your 'It' Factor...............33

    Building Your Competitive Battleground: The Power of the Matrix...............34

        Step 1: Identify the Battlefield Axes...............34

        Step 2: Gather Intel on Your Rivals...............35

        Step 3: Plot Your Position & Analyze the Landscape...............35

Analyze the landscape: ...................................................................... 35

Step 4: Charting Your Course to Victory ................................. 36

Exercise: The One-Sentence Gut Check ................................. 36

It's Not Just What You DO, But HOW You Do It ...................... 37

## Chapter 5:
## Messaging
## - Amplifying Your Voice .......................................................... 38

Why Most Brand Messaging Fails .......................................... 39

Case Study: Food Manufacturer ............................................. 40

Speak Your Customer's Language .......................................... 40

Exercise: The Billboard Test .................................................... 41

The Art of Adapting .................................................................. 41

## Chapter 6:
## Channels
## - Reaching the Untapped ....................................................... 42

Beyond the Usual Suspects .................................................... 43

Case Study: Foods Distributor ................................................ 44

The Power of Experimentation ............................................... 44

Exercise: Mapping Your Channel Expansion ......................... 44

The Content Advantage ........................................................... 45

## Chapter 7:
## Data-Driven Growth
## - Decoding Your Performance ............................................... 46

Data: Your Growth Compass ................................................... 47

Case Study: Cookware ............................................................. 48

The Right Metrics for the Right Results ................................. 48

Tools of the Trade .................................................................... 49

Exercise: The Data Dashboard..................................................49

Data Isn't Scary, It's Empowering...........................................49

## Chapter 8:
## Embracing Technology and Innovation............................50

Why Innovation Isn't Optional.................................................51

Case Study: Cookware.............................................................51

Fostering an Innovation Culture.............................................52

Innovation Hotspots..................................................................52

Exercise: The "What if...?" Session..........................................53

The Power of Partnerships......................................................53

## Chapter 9:
## Customer Experience
## - Delighting into Loyalty.....................................................54

Why Customer Experience Matters for US Brands................55

Case Study: The 'Above & Beyond' Effect..............................56

CX is About Every Touchpoint................................................56

Measuring Your CX...................................................................57

Building a CX-Focused Culture...............................................57

Exercise: The Customer Journey Empathy Map....................58

The Power of Delight................................................................58

## Chapter 10:
## Building an Agile Culture...................................................59

Why Agility Matters More Than Ever.....................................60

Case Study: The Decline of the Giant.....................................60

Building a Culture Where Change Thrives.............................61

Exercise: The Agility Audit......................................................62

A Living, Breathing Strategy................................................................62

## Chapter 11:
## The Power of Partnerships: Collaboration for Growth...............63

Why Partnerships Matter More Than Ever........................................ 64

The Partnership Playground: Choosing Your Playmates........ 65

    Model #1: The Transparent Co-Branded Alliance...............65

    Model #2: The White-Label Partnership
    (Behind-the-Scenes Collaboration)................................................ 66

    Model #3: The Strategic Joint Venture........................................ 66

    Beyond Competitors: The Power of Complementary
    Partnerships............................................................................................. 67

    Think Outside the Box:........................................................................67

    The Key to Successful Partnerships:............................................68

Case Study: The Unexpected Duo...................................................... 68

Finding the Perfect Match....................................................................... 69

The Key to Partnership Success............................................................70

Exercise: Your Partnership Dream Team............................................ 70

Ready to Collaborate................................................................................. 70

## Chapter 12:
## Financial Mastery for Success.........................................................71

Busting the P&L Myth................................................................................ 72

Case Study: The Hidden Profit Trap..................................................... 73

Essential Financial KPIs for US Growth...............................................73

Financial Tools & Habits............................................................................74

Exercise: Your Financial X-Ray................................................................74

Money as Fuel for Growth.........................................................................74

**Chapter 13:**
**The Brand Value Dashboard:**
**Your Strategy at a Glance** ............................................................. 75

    Why the BVD Matters ............................................................. 76

    Building Your BVD ................................................................... 77

    Unlocking the Power of Archetypes ..................................... 78

        Choosing Your Archetype ............................................. 80

        Using Your Archetype Powerfully ............................... 80

    Exercise: Defining Your BVD .................................................. 80

    Living with Your BVD .............................................................. 81

    Clarity is Power ........................................................................ 81

**Conclusion:**
**The Future of Your Growth Story** ................................................. 82

    A.M.P. in Action: Your Growth Playbook ............................... 83

    The Growth Never Stops ........................................................ 84

    Your Next Steps ....................................................................... 84

    Unlock Your Growth Potential with the A.M.P. Starter Kit ....... 85

        What's Inside Your Free A.M.P. Starter Kit: ............... 85

        Plus, Exclusive Access to Valuable Content: ............ 86

        How to Claim Your Free A.M.P. Starter Kit: ............... 86

        This is Just the Beginning ............................................ 86

        Let's Grow Together! ..................................................... 87

        We're Here to Help! ....................................................... 87

    The Future is Yours to Build ................................................... 87

# Preface

As the founder and CEO of Samba Rock, I've had a front-row seat to both the incredible successes and disheartening failures of international brands venturing into the US. We've partnered with remarkable companies like The Nature Conservancy, AB-Inbev (Guaraná Antarctica), Conchita Foods, and Bauducco Foods, helping them achieve remarkable growth and recognition within the US market.

My own journey spans continents and decades, shaping a unique understanding of global brand acceleration. From my early days in integrated advertising in Brazil to managing creative teams at top agencies in the UK and the US, I've honed a deep understanding of what makes brands resonate across cultures.

I used to think the biggest challenge for brands was breaking into the US market. Years of working with international companies taught me the hard truths about cultural barriers, complex distribution networks, and the sheer firepower needed to compete with established American giants.

Then, something unexpected happened. US-based brands started coming to Samba Rock. Not startups seeking a foothold, but established businesses struggling to break free from a frustrating plateau. Revenue was decent, maybe even comfortable, but that spark – that thrilling upward trajectory – had fizzled out.

At first, I was baffled. These weren't brands on the brink of failure. They had existing customer bases, brand recognition, and none of the challenges faced by companies coming in from abroad. Digging deeper, I realized the very things that fueled their initial success had turned into growth anchors.

Old marketing playbooks were collecting dust. Innovation had stalled. Assumptions about their audience were baked in, unexamined. This was the American Dream gone stale.

The A.M.P. methodology was born out of this revelation. It's a wake-up call, a diagnostic tool, and an action plan specifically designed to reignite growth for US brands. We've honed it working with companies both large and small, proving that even in a saturated market, hidden potential lies waiting to be discovered.

This isn't a book about feel-good theories. It's about rolling up your sleeves, taking an honest look at your business, and making the changes – sometimes small, sometimes radical – that lead to big results. If you're tired of settling for "good enough" and ready to reclaim your growth mojo, this book is your roadmap.

Let's shake things up, shall we?

**Valter Klug**
*Founder & CEO*
*Samba Rock Marketing Consulting*

# Introduction:
# The Great Growth Stall

Picture this: your brand was once a scrappy contender, full of ambition and big dreams. You hustled, innovated, and carved out a solid place in the US market. Revenue was flowing, customers were happy (mostly), and things felt...good.

But lately, a nagging unease has set in. Sales have plateaued. Your marketing, once fresh and exciting, feels tired and predictable. That spark of innovation that used to fuel your team has dimmed. You're coasting, not conquering.

This is the Great Growth Stall, and it's more common than you think. Many US brands, even those with years of success under their belt, hit this invisible wall. What got you here won't get you to the next level.

The frustrating part? The seeds of your growth breakthrough are likely hidden within your own business. You just need the right tools to uncover them.

That's where A.M.P. comes in. Think of it as a GPS for growth, recalibrating your strategy based on:

# Assessment: Exposing the blind spots that are holding you back.

- Mindset: Shifting from "how we've always done it" to "how can we do it better?"
- Positioning: Rediscovering your unique edge and amplifying your message in a crowded market.

# Success Story: The Sleeping Giant

We worked with a well-known US brand, a household name in its category. Yet, they were bleeding market share to newer, more agile competitors. Our A.M.P. process revealed they were resting on their laurels, overlooking shifts in consumer preferences and the untapped power of emerging social platforms. A revamped strategy, focusing on resonating with a younger demographic, revitalized the brand and reversed their decline.

This book will guide you through the A.M.P. process, step by step. It's about asking tough questions, embracing data-driven insights, and uncovering the hidden opportunities that reignite your growth trajectory.

# Chapter 1:
## **Assessment**
- Exposing Your Blind Spots

We humans are creatures of habit. This serves us well in daily life, but it's a growth-killer for businesses. What worked a few years ago probably isn't delivering the same results today. The problem is, we're often blind to our own stagnation.

The first step of the A.M.P. method is a deep-dive self-assessment, designed to shine a harsh spotlight on where you might be stuck without realizing it. This isn't about placing blame; it's about getting brutally honest so you can course-correct.

## Where Growth Goes to Die

Let's look at some common areas where growth gets stifled:

- The "We Know Our Customer" Trap: You think you know your ideal customer, but are you truly in tune with their evolving needs, pain points, and aspirations? Or are you relying on outdated assumptions?

- Siloed Thinking: Are your marketing, sales, and product teams operating in separate bubbles? This leads to disjointed messaging, missed opportunities, and an inability to adapt quickly as a whole.

- Tech & Innovation Neglect: Are you stuck with legacy systems, ignoring emerging platforms, and resistant to new ways of doing things? This is a recipe for obsolescence.

- The Sacred Cows: Every business has those untouchable elements – a tagline, a product feature, an event – that persist purely because "that's how we've always done it." Challenge everything!

## Case Study: The Missed Opportunity

A medium, established retailer with strong in-store sales but a minimal online presence. Our assessment revealed a significant revenue gap in e-commerce, and an under-investment in digital marketing compared to their competitors. This assessment was a wake-up call, leading to a major strategic shift to capture growing online market share.

## The A.M.P. Audit

It's time to turn the lens inward. Here's a structured approach:

1. Internal Audit: Gather key stakeholders from different departments. Examine your brand identity, messaging on all channels, and your organizational structure. Look for inconsistencies, redundancies, and outdated practices.

2. External Scan: Analyze market trends, competitor moves, and shifts in audience behavior. Are you keeping up, or lagging dangerously behind? Identify emerging channels and opportunities you may be missing.

## Getting into Action

To establish your baseline, take our initial A.M.P. Assessment. Ask yourself and your internal team these questions:

## Past: Your Brand's Journey

- Founding Story: When and why was your brand created? What problem did it aim to solve, and for whom?

- Major Milestones: What were the key decisions or pivots that propelled your growth?

- Lessons Learned: What strategies worked spectacularly? Which ones didn't, and why?

## Present: Where You Stand Today

- Brand Identity: In a few sentences, define what makes your brand unique.

- Competitive Landscape: Who are your primary competitors, both domestically and any you anticipate in the US market?

- Target Market: Describe your ideal customers (demographic, needs, aspirations), both in your home market and any US-specific segments you've identified.

- Growth Metrics: How do you measure success (sales, market share, awareness, etc.)? How has your performance trended in recent years?

**Future: Your US Growth Vision**

- Expansion Goals: Why expand? How does this align with your overall brand vision?

- Success Defined: What does a successful growth look like (year one, and longer term)?

- Investment Mindset: What budget range are you considering for the first year to give your growth strategy a strong foundation?

- Solving Problems: How does your brand address the unique needs/pain points of American consumers?

- Team Structure: How will you manage operations, sales, and marketing? Will this be in-house, with an agency, or a hybrid approach?

# Exercise: The 5 Whys

Pick a recent marketing campaign that underperformed. Ask "Why?" it didn't meet expectations. Then ask "Why?" again, and again, at least five times. You'll be surprised how quickly you peel back the surface to reveal deeper issues.

# Get Ready to Get Uncomfortable

This assessment process won't be a feel-good exercise. It's designed to shake things up and force you to confront the areas where you've grown complacent. But remember, discomfort is the first sign of progress.

# Chapter 2:
## Mindset
– Breaking Free from "How We've Always Done It"

You can have the most brilliant market analysis and innovative strategies, but without the right mindset, you'll get stuck in the same old patterns, yielding the same old results. The A.M.P approach is about embracing change, challenging assumptions, and fostering a culture of continuous evolution.

## The Innovation Killers

Here are some common mindset traps that stifle growth:

- Fear of Failure: Playing it safe feels comfortable, but it leads to stagnation. A growth mindset sees failure as a learning opportunity, not a catastrophe.

- The Curse of Complacency: "If it ain't broke, don't fix it," is a recipe for obsolescence. Businesses that thrive are constantly asking, "How can we make it better?"

- Resistance to Change: Change is scary, but it's the lifeblood of business. Clinging to outdated practices because "that's how we do it here" guarantees you'll be left behind.

- Ego-Driven Decision Making: Are decisions made based on what's best for the company, or what protects someone's ego or territory?

# Case Study: Hispanic Food Company

A legacy Hispanic food brand had always relied on word-of-mouth and traditional retail for growth. Recognizing the need for a change, we helped them embrace a modern marketing mindset. We shifted their focus from just selling products to building a brand story, leveraging the powerful narrative of the abuela (Hispanic grandma) that inspired the inception of the brand, 3 generations ago. This fresh approach opened up new possibilities for reaching and connecting with their growing consumer base.

## Cultivating a Growth Mindset

Here's how to shift your organization towards a mindset primed for A.M.P. success:

- Celebrate Experimentation: Encourage calculated risks, create space for testing new ideas, and reward initiative even when it doesn't yield immediate home runs.

- Data as Your Compass: Foster a data-driven culture where decisions are based on evidence, not gut feelings or outdated best practices.

- Embrace the 'Why Not?': Challenge every process, every assumption with the question "Why not do it differently?" You might be surprised at the potential you unlock.

- Hire for Curiosity: Bring in team members who are naturally inquisitive, ask insightful questions, and aren't bound by the status quo.

# Exercise: The Innovation Blindspot Audit

It's easy to get comfortable. The danger for a US-focused brand is getting too comfortable. So let's shake things up a bit:

1. List Your Offerings: Write down every product or service you currently offer.

2. Rate Your Disruption: Honestly score each offering on a scale of 1-5: 1 being 'me-too' with barely any differentiation, and 5 being a totally disruptive game-changer for your industry.

3. Radical Reimagining: If your business vanished, and you were forced to start fresh tomorrow, what would the new version look like? What bold moves would you make that you can't (or won't) do currently?

# The Power of Disruption

Disrupting yourself before the market does is the key to longevity. It's uncomfortable, but it's essential. Companies that cling to the past end up becoming case studies about what NOT to do.

# Adapting to the New Normal: Business Strategies Post-COVID-19

The pandemic wasn't just a temporary storm, it reshaped the entire business landscape. Those clinging to "how we've always done it" are going to get left behind. This is your wake-up call to not just recover, but to emerge stronger, armed with lessons learned from the global disruption.

## Key Lesson #1: Agility is the New Superpower

Remember the scramble to pivot in those early months? Overnight, businesses had to shift to remote work, rethink supply chains, and invent new ways to reach customers. The winners were those who could adapt fast – and that speed needs to become part of your DNA.

- Strategy: "Micro-Experiments Don't be afraid to test new ideas quickly, ditch what fails, and scale what works. It's better than those year-long plans that are obsolete by month two.

- Case Study: The Restaurant That Reinvented Itself A fine dining restaurant forced to close launched meal kits, online cooking classes, and even branded merch... some of those are now permanent revenue streams!

## Key Lesson #2: Digital Isn't Optional, It's the Foundation

If you weren't all-in on digital before, you are now. But it's not just a website...here's what you need:

- Frictionless E-commerce: If buying from you is clunky, they'll click away. This needs constant improvement (use your OWN website as a customer).

- Digital Community: Social media, email...this is where you build relationships directly with customers, building loyalty that can weather any storm.

- Data is Your Compass: Track more than just sales. What content resonates? Where do customers drop off? This lets you make smarter decisions, faster

## Key Lesson #3: The Human Connection Matters More Than Ever

Tech is powerful, but in times of uncertainty, people crave authentic connection more than ever.

- Empathy as a Strategy: Put yourself in your customers' shoes. What fears or unmet needs emerged from the pandemic? Can your product/service solve them in a genuine way?

- Personal Touch in a Digital World: Handwritten thank-you notes, surprise perks for loyal customers...small gestures stand out in a sea of automation.

## Resilience = Reinvention

Some businesses didn't just survive the pandemic, they thrived due to their ability to reinvent key aspects of their model. Ask yourself:

- Can your product/service be reimagined for evolving needs? A fitness studio offering outdoor classes, a retailer adding subscription boxes... necessity is the mother of innovation!

- New Channels = New Customers: Are there untapped audiences to reach online, or through strategic partnerships? Don't stay confined to your old stomping grounds.

## Health & Safety: The Trust Factor

Ignoring this is just bad business. Customers and employees need to feel confident.

- Transparency is Key: Clearly communicate protocols, even if they change over time. Don't make people guess.

- It's in the Details: Sanitizer stations, contactless options...the little things demonstrate that you care

## The World is Open for Business (Again) – Are You Ready?

Don't think of this as a return to 'normal.' There's a new landscape out there, with new expectations and opportunities. Embracing adaptability, putting people first, and building a resilient model are your keys to not just surviving, but thriving in the long run!

# Chapter 3:
## **Market Analysis**
- Seeing the Unseen

You think you know your market? Think again. Even the most thorough research gets stale over time. The A.M.P. method emphasizes revisiting your market analysis with fresh eyes, looking for the shifts and opportunities you might have missed while focused on day-to-day operations.

## Where Growth Opportunities Hide

Here's where to focus your analysis to uncover hidden potential:

- Emerging Trends: Don't just track industry news, look at adjacent markets. What innovations outside your niche could you adapt to get ahead of competitors?

- Untapped Audiences: Are you overlooking smaller customer segments with significant spending power and unmet needs? Niche audiences can fuel major growth.

- Changing Consumer Behavior: How are preferences, shopping habits, and pain points evolving? Are you adapting, or still catering to yesterday's customer?

- Competitor Blind Spots: Analyze not just what competitors do well, but where they're failing to meet customer needs. This is where you can swoop in and win market share.

# Case Study: Juice Brand

A beloved '80s juice brand had faded from popularity. Our analysis revealed a powerful, untapped trend: nostalgia for the '80s and '90s amongst younger generations. We recognized that the brand's Brooklyn roots and history aligned perfectly with the resurgence of hip hop culture, allowing us to reposition this brand in a way that deeply resonated with a new customer base.

## Data-Driven Discovery

Don't rely on gut feelings or outdated reports. Leverage these resources:

- Secondary Research: Industry reports, government statistics, consumer surveys – a treasure trove of insights that are often underutilized.

- Primary Research: Don't have the budget for extensive market research? Even small-scale surveys, focus groups, and social media polls can yield valuable data.

- Social Listening: Monitor online conversations, reviews, and competitor mentions to track real-time sentiment shifts and uncover unmet needs.

# Exercise: Crafting Your U.S. Customer Persona

You know your customers domestically, but the US market requires a new lens. Let's build a profile of your ideal US customer:

- Demographics 101: The basics: age, income, location, occupation... but tailored to US segments.

- Beyond the Basics: Dig into psychographics – lifestyles, values, online behaviors specific to US consumers. Tools like Google Trends and social listening can reveal powerful insights.

- Pain Points & Aspirations: What keeps your US customer up at night? What are their unfulfilled desires relative to products/services like yours?

## Beyond the Obvious

Surface-level analysis won't lead to breakthroughs. Dig deeper, ask the uncomfortable questions:

- Are there problems your customers have that you're NOT solving?

- What keeps them up at night that your product or service could address?

- Are you making it too easy for customers to switch to a competitor?

# Chapter 4:
## **Positioning**
- Finding Your Untapped Advantage

In a crowded market, being just "good enough" is a recipe for mediocrity. The A.M.P. method emphasizes uncovering your unique advantage – the thing that makes you the ideal (and sometimes the ONLY) solution for your target customer.

## The Problem with Blending In

Too many brands fall into the trap of trying to be everything to everyone. They end up with watered-down messaging, a generic product, and no compelling reason for customers to choose them over the competition.

## The Power of Differentiation

Here's what sets apart brands that consistently break through the noise:

- Deep Understanding of Value: They go beyond features and benefits, identifying the core emotional problem they solve for their ideal customers.

- Owning Their Niche: They embrace specialization – becoming known as THE expert for a specific type of customer or problem.

- Bold Messaging: They don't shy away from provocative, memorable messaging that cuts through the clutter and attracts their target audience like a magnet.

# Case Study: Refreshment Beverage

We took a bold approach, leaning into a beverage's past instead of trying to appear overly modern. The "New Flavors of Hip Hop" platform connected the brand to emerging hip hop artists, revitalizing its image. By embracing its unique history and authenticity, the brand became cool again, attracting a whole new generation of consumers.

# Rediscover Your 'It' Factor

Here's how to find (or rediscover) your unique positioning:

1. Understand Your Why: Go back to the reason your business exists. What problem were you founded to solve? What change were you hoping to make?

2. Customer Deep Dive: Who does your product or service make the biggest difference for? Get specific – demographics, psychographics, deepest pain points.

3. Competitive X-Ray: How are you truly different from your competitors? What gap in the market do YOU fill better than anyone else?

# Building Your Competitive Battleground: The Power of the Matrix

Now that you've taken a deep dive into your target audience and their needs (Chapter 3!), it's time to size up your competition. But how do you effectively compare yourself to a landscape of rivals, each with its own strengths and weaknesses? Enter the competitive matrix, a powerful tool to visualize your positioning and identify strategic opportunities.

Think of it like a battleground map: You are the conquering hero, and your competitors are the fortresses you need to navigate and ultimately overcome. Here's how to build your personalized competitive matrix:

## Step 1: Identify the Battlefield Axes

The magic of the matrix lies in choosing the two most relevant factors for your niche market. These axes will act as your measuring sticks, allowing you to compare yourself to your competitors head-to-head.

Here are some popular options to consider, but remember, the best choice depends on your specific industry:

- Price vs. Quality: This classic battleground pits affordability against premium offerings.
- Innovation vs. Market Share: Are you a nimble disruptor or a well-established player?
- Features vs. Ease of Use: Do you offer a feature-rich powerhouse or a user-friendly experience?
- Customization vs. Standardization: How much flexibility do you provide to your customers?

## Step 2: Gather Intel on Your Rivals

Become a competitive intelligence ninja! Research your top 3-5 competitors. What are their strengths and weaknesses? How do they position themselves in the market? Here are some resources to fuel your intel gathering:

- Competitor Websites & Social Media: Analyze their messaging and branding.

- Industry Reports & Publications: Stay up-to-date on market trends and competitor news.

- Customer Reviews & Feedback: See what customers are saying about your competitors (and you!).

## Step 3: Plot Your Position & Analyze the Landscape

Now comes the fun part! Place yourself and your competitors on the matrix based on your chosen axes. Here's where a healthy dose of self-awareness is key. Be honest about your strengths and weaknesses relative to the competition.

### Analyze the landscape:

- Are there any wide-open spaces on the matrix? This could indicate an opportunity for differentiation.

- Are you bunched up with competitors? Time to consider a strategic shift to stand out.

- Are there dominant players in certain areas? How can you avoid a head-on collision and find your niche advantage?

# Step 4: Charting Your Course to Victory

The competitive matrix is your springboard for crafting a winning strategy:

- Focus on Differentiation: Don't be a copycat! Use the matrix to identify areas where you can stand out from the crowd.

- Target the Gaps: See an unmet need in the market? This is your chance to become the hero and capture a loyal customer base.

- Develop a Clear Value Proposition: Based on your matrix insights, refine your messaging to clearly communicate what makes you unique and valuable to your target audience.

Remember, the competitive matrix is a living document. As your business evolves and the market landscape shifts, revisit your matrix regularly to ensure your positioning stays sharp and your path to US market dominance remains clear.

## Exercise: The One-Sentence Gut Check

Can you summarize your unique value proposition in a single, powerful sentence? If it takes a paragraph, you haven't found your core differentiator yet.

# It's Not Just What You DO, But HOW You Do It

Your personality, your values, your backstory – it all infuses your brand with a flavor no one else can replicate. Embrace it! This is what makes you memorable and builds customer loyalty.

# Chapter 5:
# **Messaging**
- Amplifying Your Voice

You could have the most innovative product, the best market insights, and a crystal-clear understanding of your unique advantage. But if your messaging falls flat, all that potential goes to waste. The A.M.P. method emphasizes crafting messages that resonate deeply with your target audience, making them feel seen, understood, and eager to buy.

## Why Most Brand Messaging Fails

Here's where many businesses stumble with their messaging:

- Features over Benefits: Listing product features is boring. Focus on the transformation you offer customers, paint a vivid picture of how their life improves.

- Me-Focused Messaging: Nobody cares about YOU. They care about how you solve THEIR problems and fulfill THEIR desires.

- Copycat Syndrome: Trying to imitate competitors' tone of voice makes you invisible. Your brand personality is a key part of your differentiation.

- Inconsistent Voice: If your website, social media, and ads all sound disjointed, you create a confusing (and untrustworthy) brand experience.

## Case Study: Food Manufacturer

By repositioning a Hispanic food manufacturer brand around the warmth and authenticity of abuela (the Hispanic grandma), we developed a brand voice that resonated emotionally. This storytelling approach extended across social media, email marketing, and a new website. Instead of just pushing products, this brand began sharing recipes, traditions, and the story of their family business – creating a loyal community and driving increased sales.

## Speak Your Customer's Language

Here's how to craft messaging that sticks:

- Know Your Audience Intimately: Their lingo, what keeps them up at night, their aspirations – mirror it back to them to create an instant connection.

- Emotion Trumps Logic: Yes, facts matter, but decisions are made emotionally. Tap into the deeper desires your product or service fulfills.

- Storytelling Sells: Weave narratives into your messaging. Case studies, testimonials, even your brand's origin story create powerful emotional resonance.

- Test & Adapt: No message is perfect the first time. Monitor engagement, refine, and get feedback from real customers to optimize your impact.

## Exercise: The Billboard Test

If your core value proposition had to fit on a highway billboard with only 5-7 words, what would it say? This forces you to be ruthlessly focused.

## The Art of Adapting

Different channels require different messaging approaches. Your brand voice should be consistent, but the tone, length, and focus need to adapt:

1. Social Media: Conversational, engaging, image-driven

2. Website: Clear, benefits-focused, guiding towards conversion

3. Email: Personalized, tailored to specific segments

# Chapter 6:
# **Channels**
## - Reaching the Untapped

Don't fall into the trap of "if it ain't broke, don't fix it" with your marketing channels. Even those delivering decent results for you now are likely missing out on significant segments of your target market. The A.M.P approach is about going where your ideal customers are already actively engaged, and crafting the right kind of content for those spaces.

## Beyond the Usual Suspects

Let's explore some channels often overlooked by established brands:

- Niche Online Communities: Forums, subreddits, and niche social platforms where your target audience discusses their pain points and seeks recommendations.

- Influencer Partnerships: Not just the mega-celebrities, but micro-influencers with highly engaged followings within your specific niche.

- Content as Connection: Beyond ads, create valuable, informative content (blogs, videos, guides) that establishes you as an authority and attracts customers organically.

- Strategic Partnerships: Teaming up with complementary businesses (not direct competitors) that cater to the same audience to cross-promote and expand your reach.

- Emerging Platforms: Don't be afraid of TikTok, Twitch, or whatever the next big thing might be. If your audience is there, you should be too (with content tailored to the platform).

## Case Study: Foods Distributor

To reach beyond their traditional retail base, we expanded a well known food distributor's presence to include e-commerce, launching a comprehensive Amazon strategy. This involved creating optimized listings, building an Amazon storefront, and targeted advertising campaigns. The result? A new online revenue stream and exponential expansion of their customer reach throughout the US.

## The Power of Experimentation

Here's how to strategically test new channels:

- Start Small: Don't revamp your entire strategy. Choose 1-2 new channels, allocate a modest trial budget, and track results closely.

- Match Content to the Channel: A blog post repurposed on Instagram won't perform well. Understand the unique content styles of each platform.

- Don't Get Discouraged: It takes time to build a following on new channels. Measure progress, refine your approach, and be patient.

## Exercise: Mapping Your Channel Expansion

Knowing where you are is just as important as knowing where you're going. Let's see your current marketing landscape and envision its expansion:

- Your Current Channels: List every channel you currently use to reach customers.

- Effectiveness Audit: Rate each channel's ROI (high/medium/low). Be brutally honest!

- Untapped Potential: List 3-5 channels you think could be effective for the US market, but haven't explored yet. Note a key advantage of each, and a potential challenge.

- Content Fit: For each new channel, what type of content would be most likely to succeed there? (Short-form video, long-form blogs, visuals, etc.)

# The Content Advantage

In today's crowded market, advertising alone won't cut it. Here's the A.M.P. content approach:

- Educate, Don't Sell: Answer common questions, solve problems, showcase your expertise. This builds trust and positions you as the go-to choice.

- Repurpose Strategically: A single piece of core content (like a webinar) can be turned into blog posts, social snippets, video clips, and more.

- Emphasize Quality: A few well-produced, high-value pieces are better than a flood of mediocre content.

# Chapter 7:
# Data-Driven Growth
## - Decoding Your Performance

Many businesses collect data, but few know how to turn it into actionable insights. A.M.P. puts data at the core of your strategy. It reveals what's working, what needs to change, and highlights the hidden opportunities driving growth.

## Data: Your Growth Compass

Think of data as the ultimate truth-teller. Here's why it's essential:

- Eliminate Guesswork: Gut feelings and assumptions lead you astray. Data reveals the actual impact of your marketing efforts.

- Optimize Your Spend: See exactly which channels and campaigns deliver the highest ROI, allowing you to allocate budgets wisely.

- Pinpoint Bottlenecks: Is your website turning away customers? Does a particular ad have an abysmal click-through rate? Data reveals where to fix problems.

- Spot Emerging Trends: Monitoring the right metrics helps you react quickly to market shifts and capitalize on new opportunities before competitors.

# Case Study: Cookware

Cookware company X's outdated, sales-focused website was failing to convert visitors. Data analysis revealed poor user experience and a lack of trust-building elements. We revitalized the site, incorporating modern design and a more consumer-centric approach. This led to a surge in both new customer acquisition and increased interest in becoming resellers, driving significant online sales growth.

## The Right Metrics for the Right Results

Don't get lost in a sea of data. Focus on the key metrics that align with your goals:

- Sales & Revenue: The ultimate measure of success, but be sure to track where growth is coming from (which channels, campaigns, etc.).

- Website Traffic & Engagement: Shows how well your content and marketing are attracting and keeping visitors' attention.

- Lead Generation: Vital for B2B businesses. Are you attracting qualified leads that are likely to convert into customers?

- Customer Lifetime Value: Helps you make strategic decisions about how much you're willing to spend to acquire a new customer.

## Tools of the Trade

Here's where to get your data, and how to make sense of it:

- Website Analytics: Google Analytics is essential, but may require expertise to interpret effectively.

- Social Media Insights: Built-in analytics tools on most platforms provide valuable data about engagement and audience demographics.

- CRM: Your customer relationship management system is a treasure trove of data about customer behavior and buying patterns.

- A/B Testing Tools: Test different headlines, CTAs, images, etc. to see what your audience responds to best.

## Exercise: The Data Dashboard

Identify the top 5 metrics most important to your current business goals. Create a simple dashboard (spreadsheet is fine for starters) to track these weekly at a minimum.

## Data Isn't Scary, It's Empowering

Don't be intimidated by data analysis! Start simple, and as you get comfortable, you can dive deeper. Look for patterns, anomalies, and connections between different metrics. The insights you uncover will fuel your growth.

# Chapter 8:
# Embracing Technology and Innovation

Stagnation is the enemy of growth. The A.M.P. method emphasizes continuous innovation – embracing new technologies, finding fresh ways to solve problems, and always looking for the next way to better serve your customers.

## Why Innovation Isn't Optional

Here's why established businesses MUST focus on innovation:

- Disrupt or Be Disrupted: Startups and agile competitors are constantly pushing boundaries. If you're not doing the same, you'll be left in the dust.

- Customer Expectations Evolve: What wowed customers a few years ago is table stakes today. Keep raising the bar on experience and value.

- New Tech = New Opportunities: AI, automation, virtual reality... these aren't just buzzwords. Harness them to streamline operations, improve customer experience, and gain a competitive edge.

## Case Study: Cookware

By recognizing the power of a well-designed, optimized website, a renowned cookware manufacturer was able to transform its digital presence. This modernization, coupled with a refreshed brand identity, opened up new revenue streams and positioned the brand as a forward-thinking leader within its niche.

# Fostering an Innovation Culture

How to make innovation a core part of your company DNA:

- Lead from the Top: If leaders aren't excited about new ideas, employees won't be either. Champion a continuous improvement mindset.

- R&D Doesn't Have to Be Expensive: Start with small, focused experiments. Set aside a modest budget for testing new technology or processes.

- Get Out of Your Bubble: Attend industry events, network outside your niche, and study how businesses in other sectors are innovating.

- Encourage Curiosity: Give employees time and space to explore new ideas, even if they seem outside their job description.

# Innovation Hotspots

Where should you be looking for innovation opportunities?

- Customer Pain Points: What keeps your customers up at night? Can you develop new products, services, or processes that make their lives easier?

- Internal Bottlenecks: Are outdated systems and inefficient workflows slowing you down? Look for tech solutions to streamline and automate.

- Emerging Trends: Monitor not just your industry, but adjacent markets. What innovations could you adapt to give you an edge?

## Exercise: The "What if...?" Session

Challenge your team to come up with the craziest, most out-there ideas. Even seemingly unrealistic solutions can spark a more practical, innovative approach.

## The Power of Partnerships

You don't have to innovate in a vacuum. Collaborate with:

- Tech Startups: Tap into cutting-edge technology without major in-house development costs.

- Complementary Businesses: Develop joint offerings that expand both of your customer bases.

# Chapter 9:
## Customer Experience
- Delighting into Loyalty

Acquiring new customers is expensive. Delivering an exceptional customer experience is the key to turning them into repeat buyers, powerful advocates, and a major engine for sustainable growth.

## Why Customer Experience Matters for US Brands

Let's face it, US companies aren't always known for stellar customer service. This creates a huge opportunity for your brand to stand out. Here's why focusing on CX is your secret weapon:

- Word-of-Mouth Wins: Happy customers become your marketing team, sharing positive experiences and driving organic growth.

- Increased Lifetime Value: Loyal customers spend more and are more tolerant of the occasional price increase

- Competitive Advantage: Even if a competitor copies your product, they can't replicate the feeling customers get interacting with your brand.

- Resilience During Tough Times: Loyal customers are more forgiving of the occasional mistake if your overall CX is excellent.

# Case Study: The 'Above & Beyond' Effect

Once upon a time there was a mid-sized consumer goods company with decent customer satisfaction ratings, but lackluster growth. They developed a comprehensive customer experience audit that identified friction points across the purchase journey, hindering repeat purchases. Small but impactful changes in the post-sale experience (packaging, follow-up, etc.) significantly increased customer satisfaction and repeat orders.

## CX is About Every Touchpoint

Here's where to focus to optimize your customer experience:

- First Impressions Count: Is your website easy to navigate, messaging clear, and the buying process seamless?

- Responsive Support: Do customers get timely, helpful responses to questions and issues?

- The Human Element: Even with technology, don't lose sight of personalized, empathetic interactions that build relationships.

- Anticipating Needs: Can you proactively address common problems or offer surprise upgrades and exclusive perks?

# Measuring Your CX

Here's how to know if your efforts are paying off:

- Net Promoter Score (NPS): A simple metric for gauging how likely customers are to recommend you.

- Customer Reviews: Monitor online reviews for patterns of praise and complaints.

- Churn Rate: How many customers are you losing over time? High churn points to CX problems.

- Qualitative Feedback: Conduct regular surveys or focus groups to get rich insights directly from customers.

# Building a CX-Focused Culture

Here's how to make this part of your company DNA:

- Hire for Empathy: Caring about customers should be a top priority, even beyond specific skills.

- Empower Employees: Give them the tools and autonomy to solve customer problems on the spot, without escalating every issue.

- CX Champions: Identify individuals within your team who are passionate about delighting customers, and make them role models for others.

# Exercise: The Customer Journey Empathy Map

Step into your customer's shoes to unlock the path to loyalty. Here's how:

- Map the Journey: Outline every interaction a US customer has with your brand. Be granular! From the first ad they see, to the purchase process, to the unboxing experience, to follow-up communication.

- Pain & Delight: At each step of the journey, honestly note where customers might experience frustration and where they are delighted by something you do exceptionally well.

- CX Transformation: Pick ONE pain point to solve. Brainstorm at least 5 solutions, ranging from practical improvements to truly unique ways of exceeding customer expectations.

## The Power of Delight

Don't settle for "good enough" customer experience. Aim to create moments that make customers feel valued, understood, and excited to keep returning to your brand.

# Chapter 10:
# Building an Agile Culture

The most dangerous word for an established business is "complacency." Even with a strong track record, failing to adapt to a dynamic market is a recipe for obsolescence. The A.M.P. approach isn't about a one-time fix. It's about instilling a culture of continuous adaptation, where embracing change and experimentation becomes part of your company's DNA.

## Why Agility Matters More Than Ever

Here's why US brands specifically need to prioritize agility:

- Constant Market Disruption: The US market is a hotbed of innovation. Startups, tech giants, and even changing consumer preferences disrupt the status quo constantly.

- Customer Expectations Evolve: What satisfied customers yesterday is merely table stakes today. Agile businesses stay one step ahead, anticipating and exceeding evolving needs.

- Opportunities are Fleeting: In this fast-paced market, the ability to capitalize on emerging trends quickly separates winners from those left behind.

## Case Study: The Decline of the Giant

A traditional manufacturing company struggling to keep pace with changing market demands due to slow decision-making and siloed departments. We helped them implement a cross-functional "sprint" structure, encouraging rapid prototyping and iteration. This empowered teams to respond to customer feedback in real-time, leading to faster product development and increased market responsiveness.

# Building a Culture Where Change Thrives

Here's how to make agility a core part of how your company operates:

- Mindset Shift: Foster a fearlessness of failure. Reward smart risks and celebrate learning from missteps. Communicate that standing still is far riskier than trying and adapting.

- Data-Driven Experimentation: Encourage running small tests at every level of the organization. Measure outcomes, iterate ruthlessly, and scale what works.

- Cross-Functional Teams: Break down silos! Collaboration between marketing, sales, product, and customer service sparks innovation and allows for quick pivots based on market response.

- Hire for Curiosity: Look beyond skill sets. Employees who are naturally inquisitive, ask great questions, and aren't afraid of the unknown will drive your agile culture.

- Empowered Employees: Give your team the freedom and mandate to make decisions within their domains. Trust is crucial for rapid response to market signals.

## Exercise: The Agility Audit

How agile is your company right now? Rate yourselves on a scale of 1 (rigid) to 5 (highly adaptive) for these areas:

- Speed of decision-making
- Willingness to experiment
- Cross-team communication
- Response to competitor actions
- Customer feedback integration

## A Living, Breathing Strategy

The A.M.P. methodology, by nature, helps you become more agile. Consistent assessments, market analysis, and a data-driven approach ensure you're never complacent, always adapting, and constantly unlocking new growth opportunities in the ever-evolving US market.

# Chapter 11:
## The Power of Partnerships:
Collaboration for Growth

In the past, businesses often saw themselves as solitary islands, fighting fiercely for market share. But the US market rewards a more collaborative mindset. Strategic partnerships can unlock growth opportunities that simply aren't possible alone. Let's redefine how you think about collaboration and explore the powerful partnerships that can fuel your US success.

## Why Partnerships Matter More Than Ever

Here's why forming strong partnerships is key for US-focused brands:

- Speed & Agility: The US market demands fast action. Partnering allows you to access resources, expertise, and reach without building everything in-house.

- Reduced Risk: Partnering with established US businesses or specialists reduces market entry risk, leveraging their experience and local knowledge.

- Innovation Catalyst: Collaborating brings in fresh perspectives, pushing boundaries and sparking innovation that wouldn't happen in isolation.

- Customer Value Multiplier: The right partnerships can enhance your existing offerings, surprising and delighting customers with a more integrated experience.

# The Partnership Playground: Choosing Your Playmates

You've identified the power of collaboration, but not all partnerships are created equal. Just like choosing the right friends, selecting the ideal partner is crucial for maximizing growth. Here's a breakdown of some common partnership models, along with their pros and cons:

## Model #1: The Transparent Co-Branded Alliance

**Pros:**

- Shared resources and marketing reach: Amplify your message to a wider audience.

- Builds trust and credibility: Partnering with a reputable brand strengthens yours.

- Increased brand awareness: Cross-promotion exposes you to new customer segments.

**Cons:**

- Requires transparency and open communication: Both partners need to be aligned on goals and messaging.

- Success relies on strong brand fit: Ensure your target audiences and brand values complement each other.

- Profit sharing can be complex: Clearly define how revenue and expenses will be divided.

## Model #2: The White-Label Partnership (Behind-the-Scenes Collaboration)

**Pros:**

- Faster market entry: Leverage your partner's existing infrastructure and expertise.
- Scalability: Your partner handles production/services, allowing you to focus on sales and marketing.
- Flexibility: You can "white-label" different products/services based on market demand.

**Cons:**

- Reduced brand control: Your involvement might not be readily apparent to the customer.
- Less profit margin: You may receive a wholesale price on the service/product.
- Limited customer data access: You might not have direct access to customer information.

## Model #3: The Strategic Joint Venture

**Pros:**

- Shared risks and rewards: Partners pool resources for a high-potential project.
- Combined expertise: Leverage each other's strengths to create a powerful offering.
- Access to new markets and technologies: Partners can open doors previously closed.

**Cons:**

- Complex legal setup: Requires a formal agreement outlining ownership, responsibilities, and exit strategies.

- Potential for disagreements: Strong communication and conflict resolution skills are crucial.

- Longer time to market: Getting everything aligned between two companies can take time.

## Beyond Competitors: The Power of Complementary Partnerships

Traditionally, we've viewed peers as rivals. But the A.M.P. mindset flips that script. Let's say you're a bakery known for incredible cakes. Partnering with a local coffee shop for a "Cake & Coffee" combo can be mutually beneficial. You don't compete, you complement each other, creating a more attractive offering for the customer and driving sales for both businesses.

## Think Outside the Box:

Don't limit yourself to partnerships within your industry. Explore collaborations with seemingly unrelated businesses. A fitness studio partnering with a clothing store for a workout apparel line, or a financial advisor teaming up with a realtor for "Wealth & Homeownership" workshops... the possibilities are endless!

## The Key to Successful Partnerships:

Remember, a successful partnership requires more than just a signed agreement. Here are success factors to keep in mind:

- Shared Vision and Values: Do your core beliefs and goals align?
- Open Communication: Transparency and honesty are essential for building trust.
- Clearly Defined Roles & Responsibilities: Who does what? Be specific to avoid confusion.
- Win-Win Mentality: Both partners should benefit from the collaboration.

By choosing the right model and fostering a strong partnership, you can unlock exponential growth opportunities. Remember, collaboration is not a weakness, it's a strategic power move!

## Case Study: The Unexpected Duo

Martha Stewart x Snoop Dogg: The unlikely pairing of the domestic lifestyle icon and the rap legend on a cooking show captivated audiences. The show's humor, authenticity, and surprising chemistry between the hosts made it a pop culture phenomenon.

## Finding the Perfect Match

Here's your partnership playbook – types to consider, and how to pick the right ones:

- Complementary Offerings: Companies with products/services that solve adjacent problems for the same target customer. Combining forces creates a seamless customer experience.

- Shared Audience: Partner with brands whose audience overlaps with yours, but you're not direct competitors. This allows access to a whole new pool of potential customers.

- Expertise Exchange: Partner with specialists to fill gaps in your team. Digital marketing agencies, logistics providers, and local market experts can boost capacity fast.

- Co-branding Magic: Collaborate on a limited-edition product, campaign, or event with another respected brand to increase reach and generate buzz for BOTH involved.

## The Key to Partnership Success

Partnership isn't just signing a contract. Here's how to make collaborations thrive:

- Shared Values: Alignment on values and company culture is crucial for synergy.
- Clear Expectations: Outline goals, responsibilities, and success metrics upfront.
- Open Communication: Regular check-ins, and honesty about challenges, builds trust.
- Win-Win Mentality: Both partners need to see clear value in the collaboration.

## Exercise: Your Partnership Dream Team

Dream big! List 3 brands that would be ideal partners to accelerate your US growth. For each, describe the unique value the partnership would create for both your brand AND your target customers.

## Ready to Collaborate

In a hyper-connected business landscape, the old 'lone wolf' mentality is a recipe for stagnation. Open your mind to a partnership-driven approach, and discover the transformative growth opportunities it unlocks for your US expansion.

# Chapter 12:
# Financial Mastery for Success

Financial blind spots can sink even the most promising US venture. Traditional accounting methods often disguise the true health of your business, especially for owner-operated brands aiming for expansion. In this chapter, we'll unpack key metrics that matter, and techniques to ensure you're making financially sound decisions for long-term success.

## Busting the P&L Myth

The Profit & Loss (P&L) statement is important, but it doesn't tell the whole story for US-focused brands. Let's introduce two powerful metrics:

- Real Revenue: Many businesses, especially agencies and service providers, handle "pass-through" costs. This means money that comes in, but is immediately paid out to vendors, platforms, etc. While it inflates your top-line revenue, it doesn't represent your true earnings power. Calculating Real Revenue (Total Revenue minus pass-through costs) gives a clearer picture of your business's profitability.

- Real Profit  Owner-operated businesses often rely on profit distributions for personal income. This disguises true financial performance. Tracking profit before distributions offers a reality check. Are you reinvesting enough back into your business for sustainable growth? A healthy US expansion requires a strong financial foundation.

# Case Study: The Hidden Profit Trap

Back in Samba Rock's scrappy early days, when I was more freelancer than CEO, I'd squeeze out a tiny salary and pat myself on the back for a "profitable" first year. But the truth was, I was barely keeping the lights on! This false sense of profitability works when you're bootstrapping, but it can become a dangerous illusion as your business grows. Let's unravel this common financial pitfall so you don't fall into the same trap!

# Essential Financial KPIs for US Growth

Beyond Real Revenue and Real Profit, here are key metrics to watch:

- Gross Margin: Measures profitability at a product/service level. Crucial for pricing strategy, especially considering US market competition and costs.

- Customer Acquisition Cost (CAC): How much does it cost to gain one new US customer? Monitoring this against Customer Lifetime Value (CLTV) reveals marketing efficiency.

- Burn Rate: How fast are you spending cash reserves? Essential for runway planning, especially during early days in the US market.

- Operational Efficiency: Track key ratios (e.g., overhead as a % of Real Revenue) to identify areas for cost savings, freeing up funds for growth initiatives.

# Financial Tools & Habits

Here's how to master your money for US expansion:

- Clean & Clear Bookkeeping: Accurate, up-to-date financial records are non-negotiable. Invest in the right software and processes (or a good bookkeeper!)

- Regular Reviews: Don't just look at financials at tax time. Monthly or quarterly reviews allow for proactive course correction.

- Scenario Planning: Model different growth scenarios (best case vs. conservative) to understand your financing needs and risk tolerance.

- Embrace the Advisor: A US-based accountant, fractional CFO, or trusted advisor can be worth their weight in gold in navigating market-specific financial complexities.

## Exercise: Your Financial X-Ray

Calculate your Real Revenue and Real Profit per quarter over the last 12 months. Is there a significant difference? How does this change your outlook? Next, pick ONE additional KPI from the list above, and set up a system to track it going forward.

## Money as Fuel for Growth

Don't let financials intimidate you. A clear-eyed view of your numbers provides the roadmap for strategic investments, responsible growth decisions, and ultimately, sustained success in the demanding US market.

# Chapter 13:
## The Brand Value Dashboard:
Your Strategy at a Glance

You've done the hard work of assessment, market analysis, and crafting a powerful US growth strategy. But how do you ensure your vision stays focused while keeping your entire team aligned? The Brand Value Dashboard (BVD) is a visual tool that distills your core brand strategy onto a single page, creating clarity and actionable direction for everyone involved in your US expansion.

## Why the BVD Matters

- Alignment: The BVD ensures every member of your team, from marketers to sales reps, understands the essence of your brand, and how their work contributes to the bigger picture.

- Focus: It's easy to get lost in daily tactics. The BVD keeps your strategic North Star in view, allowing for better prioritization and decision-making.

- Adaptability: While core brand elements should remain consistent, the BVD helps you adapt quickly to market shifts while maintaining a consistent brand experience.

# Building Your BVD

Here's a breakdown of the key components and how to craft each element:

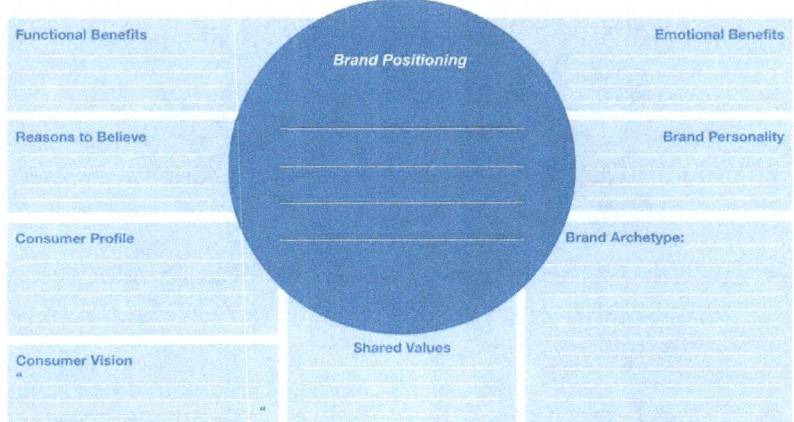

- Center: Brand Logo & Positioning The heart of your BVD. Your logo is a visual reminder, while your positioning statement (developed in Chapter 4) captures what you stand for in just a few sentences.

- Functional Benefits (Top Left): What tangible problems does your product/service solve for customers? Be specific and US-focused.

- Emotional Benefits (Top Right): How does your brand make customers FEEL? Desired emotions should connect to your target audience's aspirations (think: confident, empowered, etc.)

77

- Reasons to Believe (Middle Left): What proof backs up your claims? Awards, testimonials, unique capabilities...this builds trust.

- Brand Personality (Middle Right): If your brand was a person, how would it be described? Choose 3-5 relevant adjectives (daring, nurturing, playful...)

- Consumer Profile & Visions (Bottom Left): A sketch of your ideal US customer (from Chapter 3). "Visions" is a powerful quote summarizing what this customer wants from a brand like yours.

- Shared Values (Bottom Center): What core values do you truly SHARE with your ideal customers? This creates a powerful emotional connection.

- Brand Archetype (Bottom Right): Every strong brand taps into a universal human story. Archetypes are like timeless characters that audiences subconsciously connect with on a deep level. Understanding your brand archetype helps you craft messaging, visuals, and experiences that resonate powerfully. Which archetype best embodies your brand's essence?

## Unlocking the Power of Archetypes

Carl Jung, the famed psychologist, theorized that humans share a collective unconscious filled with primal symbols and patterns. Brand archetypes tap into these universally understood roles, making your story instantly relatable. Here's a breakdown of the 12 common archetypes:

- **The Hero:** Bold, courageous, overcomes challenges. (Examples: Nike, Red Bull)

- **The Outlaw:** Challenges the status quo, disrupts the norm. (Examples: Harley Davidson, Virgin)

- **The Magician:** Transformative, makes dreams reality. (Examples: Apple, Disney)

- **The Everyman:** Relatable, down-to-earth, champions belonging. (Examples: Dove, IKEA)

- **The Explorer:** Craves adventure, seeks new experiences. (Examples: The North Face, Jeep)

- **The Lover:** Seeks connection, driven by passion and intimacy. (Example: Chanel, Victoria's Secret)

- **The Jester:** Playful, brings joy, doesn't take things too seriously. (Examples: Old Spice, M&Ms)

- **The Caregiver:** Nurturing, protective, puts others first. (Examples: Johnson & Johnson, Campbell's Soup)

- **The Ruler:** Exudes control, commands authority, creates order. (Examples: Rolex, Microsoft)

- **The Creator:** Driven by imagination, brings new things to life. (Example: Lego, Adobe)

- **The Innocent:** Optimistic, pure, seeks a simpler, happier world. (Example: Coca-Cola, Nintendo)

- **The Sage:** Shares wisdom, values knowledge, guides others. (Examples: Google, TED Talks)

## Choosing Your Archetype

Think about the role your brand plays in your customers' lives. Do you help them overcome a struggle (Hero)? Do you inspire them to think differently (Magician)? Don't force a fit. Your primary archetype should feel authentic to your brand's core mission.

## Using Your Archetype Powerfully

Your archetype informs everything about your brand:

- Messaging: The language you use (bold vs. comforting, playful vs. authoritative)

- Visuals: The imagery, colors, and overall design aesthetic

- Brand Experiences: How you interact with customers and the overall vibe you create

# Exercise: Defining Your BVD

- Start Simple: Use sticky notes or a whiteboard to draft the content for each BVD section.

- Iterate & Refine: Get feedback from team members. Aim for brevity and impact in each section.

- Design Matters: Once your content is finalized, invest in a visually appealing design that can be proudly shared internally and with partners.

- Download a blank template of the BVD at sambarock.us/amp.

## Living with Your BVD

- Put it Front & Center: Display your BVD prominently in meeting spaces, or make it your desktop wallpaper. Daily exposure keeps it top of mind.

- Review & Refresh: Schedule quarterly check-ins with your BVD. Does it still accurately reflect your brand in the evolving US market? Updates may be needed!

## Clarity is Power

The BVD is a potent tool for achieving your US brand growth ambitions. By capturing the essence of your strategy in a visual, actionable way, you ensure focus, alignment, and adaptability – the key ingredients for long-term success.

# Conclusion:
# The Future of Your Growth Story

You've embarked on a powerful journey. The A.M.P. method has given you the tools to break free from stagnation, rediscover your potential, and ignite the next chapter of explosive growth for your brand. Remember, transformation isn't easy, but with a commitment to continuous improvement, the rewards are limitless.

## A.M.P. in Action: Your Growth Playbook

Let's recap the core principles that will now guide your strategy:

- Assessment is Power: Maintain a regular cadence of honest self-assessment, even when things are going well. Be ruthlessly honest about your blind spots.

- Mindset of Innovation: Embrace calculated risks, challenge the status quo, and foster a culture where curiosity and experimentation are rewarded.

- Market Mastery: Never stop researching and analyzing your market. Uncover the hidden trends and evolving customer needs that drive growth.

- Find Your Untapped Advantage: Own your unique value proposition and niche. Boldly communicate what sets you apart.

- Messaging that Connects: Use the language of your ideal customer, tap into their emotions, and tell stories that resonate.

- Go Where Your Customers Are: Expand your presence across platforms where your audience actively engages. Become known for valuable and informative content.

- Data-Driven Decisions: Make data analysis a cornerstone of your strategy. Use insights to optimize every aspect of your business.

- Innovation Edge: Actively seek new technologies and processes that streamline operations, improve efficiency, and surprise and delight customers.

- CX Obsession: Customer experience is where you gain a true competitive advantage. Proactively exceed your customers' expectations.

## The Growth Never Stops

The A.M.P. approach isn't a one-time fix. It's a mindset shift, a commitment to evolving along with the market. The businesses that thrive in the long run remain adaptable, customer-focused, and relentlessly driven to find new ways to be better.

## Your Next Steps

The journey to conquering the US market has just begun! This book has equipped you with the A.M.P. tools and mindset to unlock your growth potential. But remember, strategy is best put into practice. To help you turn knowledge into action, we've created a treasure trove of downloadable templates, fillable charts, and the in-depth exercises featured throughout the book. Visit us at sambarock.us/amp to access these free resources and continue your US brand growth journey.

Here's a starting point for your continued growth journey:

1. Choose ONE Area to Focus On: Pick the chapter of this book that resonated with you most. Identify specific action steps you'll take.

2. Revisit Your Assessment: In 6 months, re-do the A.M.P. audit to identify new areas for improvement and uncover additional growth potential.

3. Seek Outside Expertise: For more complex challenges, consider partnering with experienced consultants (like Samba Rock!) to accelerate and deepen your A.M.P. transformation.

# Unlock Your Growth Potential with the A.M.P. Starter Kit

You've unlocked valuable insights within this book, but the A.M.P. journey doesn't end here. To keep the momentum going, I've created a powerful A.M.P. Starter Kit packed with downloadable resources designed to jumpstart your growth!

What's Inside Your Free A.M.P. Starter Kit:

- The A.M.P. Launch Checklist: A step-by-step roadmap to guide you through the initial stages of implementing the A.M.P. framework in your business.

- The Growth Assessment Cheat Sheet: Identify your business's biggest growth opportunities – fast! This cheat sheet helps you pinpoint areas for immediate improvement.

- Customer Empathy Template: Craft a powerful customer persona to ensure your product or service resonates deeply with your target audience.

## Plus, Exclusive Access to Valuable Content:

By downloading your A.M.P. Starter Kit, you'll also be subscribed to our growth newsletter, packed with:

- Actionable Tips & Strategies: Learn how to overcome common growth hurdles and unlock hidden potential within your business.

- Inspiring Case Studies: See how real companies have used the A.M.P. method to achieve remarkable results.

- Early Access to New Resources: Be the first to know about new tools, templates, and webinars designed to fuel your growth journey.

## How to Claim Your Free A.M.P. Starter Kit:

It's simple! Just head over to sambarock.us/amp and enter your contact information. You'll receive instant access to your downloadable resources and be subscribed to our growth newsletter.

## This is Just the Beginning...

The A.M.P. Starter Kit is your springboard to a world of growth possibilities. While these resources are powerful on their own, there's a whole A.M.P. ecosystem waiting to be explored!

## Let's Grow Together!

Download your free A.M.P. Starter Kit today and unlock the growth potential within your business. With these resources and our ongoing support, you'll be well on your way to achieving remarkable results.

## We're Here to Help!

Have questions or need help getting started? Don't hesitate to reach out to our team at contact@sambarock.us. We're here to support you on your growth journey.

## The Future is Yours to Build

The US market remains a land of vast opportunity. With a combination of self-awareness, a commitment to innovation, and the tools you've gained throughout this book, you can unlock new levels of success. Your brand has the potential to become not just a household name, but a beloved part of your customers' lives.

Let your growth story continue!

www.ingramcontent.com/pod-product-compliance
Lightning Source LLC
Chambersburg PA
CBHW070350230526
45471CB00006B/2504